Walls

Don't you think it's time
That we both settle down
In a quiet little town
Beside the sea

The sky seems to be falling
And this road we keep on walking
We'll find a way to shelter from the rain

But You and I don't know
This road and where it goes
And honesty seems to go along way
So let me know you're safe
And we'll reach for a better place
And in my heart we will always stay

But it's a little late for promises
And time seems to be robbing us
of a life I know that we should have lived
when the world runs out of answers
I'll climb this Rocky ladder
and reach over this wall that's in the way

Don't you think it's time
that we both settle down
in a quiet little town and ride the train
It's been Cloudy in the morning
 And this road we keep on walking
We'll find a way to shelter from the rain

But You and I Both don't know
This road and where it goes
Or how much sunlight is left today
So let me know you're safe
 And will reach for a better place
In my heart we will always stay

But It's a little late for promises
 And time seems to be robbing us
 Of a life I know that we should have lived
 When the world runs out of answers
 and whatever fate will hand us

I will reach over this wall it's in the way

Don't you think this time
that we both settle down
in a quiet little town beside the sea

Eternity:

Water falls upon my face
As rain clouds shed a tear
All I have is who you are
Are all I hope there's you are near

I wait here a setting sun
For you to see me so
A penny for your thoughts
for a southern breeze to blow

And time is an Eternity
It was painted on the walls
Near city streets and payment tiles
Were the summer meets the fall
And for it is and we must trust
Another night to bide

Our dreams of truth a rising moon
Forever is a long long time

And words of wise
They tell the tale
That never seems to call
For we once were the destitute
And fate will write the law
We wonder the Pacific sky
As the Sun light turns it's back

As a cold dark nights will hide the moon
As the trees will turn to black

And time is an eternity
It was painted on the streets
Near city walls and payment tiles
To turn the grey complete

And for it is and we must trust
Another year to bide
Our dreams of truth
A rising moon
Forever is a long long time
Forever never dies
Forever I shall wait
An Eternity of moon and stars

forever I shall wait

Forever is a broken mile
Forever is eternal fate
A Destiny of moons and stars
Forever I shall wait

And time is an eternity
It was painted on the walls
Near city streets and payment Tiles
Where the sun light meets the fall

And for it is and we must trust
Another year to bid
Our dreams of truth a rising moon.
Forever is a long long time
Forever is a long-lived time
Forever is the question why

Forever You:

For you are my truth
My heart forever you
Daylight in my eyes
A sunset painted sky

Valleys, distant Hills
Follow nights of still
Coloured sands of time
I paint you in my mind

I need you now again
A compass to the sea
Eternal shores, open doors like a feather to the breeze
Stay with me once more, forever I adore
Your smile, your grace, your eyes
For you I'd wait the tides

My heart falls upon the waves
My heart must guide the end of the days

For I wait to see you through my mind
Will travel through time
My heart crossed the sea and the sands
Through hills and distant lands
Forever more unlocks the door to grace your hand in mine

For you are my truth
My heart forever you
The nights will surely bide
My moon will move the tide

The clock upon our wall
Eternal evermore
Sheets of times in lace
Eternal forever grace

With you
Forever you
Forever You

Waters and Waves. PI

You won't find me out in the big city
There's allot of shame
It's allot of pitty
You'll find me out in small town near the water and waves
Some people tell me I've been wasting my life
You gotta have some kids
you gotta get a wife
But it takes a while out here near the waters and waves

And life's a funny thing
You meet strangers down the road
Everywhere you go
And they all got a lot of things to say
Out here near the water is in waves

The sun beats down on my burnt back
I wish the road would cut me some slack
There's not allot going on down here near the waters and waves

And out here its gets pretty lonely
And I miss my baby back home in the big city
you gotta find some things to do from day to day

But as long as I got my guitar in my hand
And as long as I got the earth in the land
As long as the got the beaches to see the sand and the waters in waves

I'll sit here and sing my song
For how long I don't know for how long
But you know it'll be doing
I'll be seeing the sand the earth and the waves

Waters and Waves: PII

I spent the days of my youth trying to cope
With a whisky in hand and a fire to stoke
I feel the midday sun burning on my back again

I spend my nights on the road trying to shield
The cold dark clouds, fall in the field
That hide the moonlight I search for everyday

I travelled the road switching gears
The road less Travelled from years and years
And if I find another way I'll tell you everyday

And days of old will forever be
A certain clue, a destiny
A place in time that we will always stay

So wait for me, wait for us
Hold on to a place that we can trust
Where the wind is calm out here near the water and waves

Near the waters and waves
Near the waters and waves

Train wreck:

I'm packing in
I'm sipping blood
I'll take this fire out to the flood

I'm a rolling dice
my bones are aching
The storm is here no prisoners taken

Fire and Flames
You join the cult
Enjoy the pain like a lightning bolt

No end in sight
Have no fear
The spiders bite so hold my beer

I'm at Deadset Train wreck
Straight through the fire off the eastern coast off the eastern coast
I'm at Deadset Train wreck
Straight through the fire off the western coast off the western coast

I'm packing in
I'm sitting blood
I'll take this fire out to the flood

I'm a rolling dice
I'm flipping cards
I'm shaking whisky in the bar

There ain't no shame
If you join a mistaken
Guilty game of the Cult of Satan

I'm at Deadset Train wreck
Straight through the fire off the eastern coast off the eastern coast
I'm at Deadset Train wreck
Straight through the fire off the western coast off the western coast

I'm at Deadset Train wreck
Straight through the fire off the eastern coast off the eastern coast
I'm at Deadset Train wreck
Straight through the fire off the western coast off the western coast

Tides of San Diego:
I left my heart in San Diego
Packed my bags and hit the road
To a small old town by the mountains
With my heart to bear and load

She whispers me from San Diego
Golden hair and eyes of blue
From time to time I would set her free
Down by the caribou

I think about her all the time near the tide the San Diego
That's where my heart resides
I think about her every night near the tide the San Diego
I think about her as the years and waves roll by

I left my heart in San Diego
Pack my bags and filled the tank
to a small old town by the mountains
to share a beer with hank

I wandered round from year-to-year
Wasting light and talking cheap
Until the flood gates shut sometimes
And I never seemed to earn my keep

I think about her all the time near the tide the San Diego
That's where my heart resides
I think about her every night near the tide the San Diego
I think about her as the years and waves roll by

I Play Every Song For You:

I play every song for you
Baby it's you and me
And if they don't like it
It's time to set them free

Sometimes life's full of heartache
Sometimes we just survive
With you baby most of the time it's good to be alive

And I damn well won't back down

There's always another song
There's always another chance
And if you don't mind babe
I'd like your hand to dance

We tiptoe on the clouds
Sometimes just fall back down
But don't you worry about a thing
Because I play every song for you

There's always another chance
There's always another song
And sometimes I just don't know why people don't get along
It's getting kind of loud
And rowdy in the crowd
With my flag to bear
My cross to wear
My father would be proud

And I damn well won't back down

There's always another song
There's always another chance
And if you don't mind babe
I'd like your hand to dance

We tiptoe on the clouds
Sometimes just fall back down
But don't you worry about a thing
Because I play every song for you

Out here in the cold
I wanna stay with you 'till we're grey and old

There's always another song
There's always another chance
And if you don't mind babe
I'd like your hand to dance

We tiptoe on the clouds
Sometimes just fall back down
But don't you worry about a thing
Because I play every song for you

Huckleberry Finn (Letters to Heaven)

Hi Dad it's me
I'm sure you're quite aware
It's been a long old year
I know you're somewhere out there

I kind of made a mess of things
I'm not sure who to blame
But life is getting short
And I'm going quiet insane

Forgive me Dad I think of you every single day
Next time I know I'm doing wrong
I know who to blame

Forgive me Dad I think of you every single year
Next time I know I'm doing wrong
I'll walk right through the fear

My daughters far away
I'm going straight through hell
The one that thought that I had
Is empty by the shelf

I kind of think some pity
Will give me courage to myself
But life is getting long
A mental messing hell

So if I make it through this week
I'll be one of myself
I fear the anger my bones, my skin
My father's messing hands

And I don't know where the truth will messing lie
When I get my faith ill make it right

In another life
I will make it on my own
But when you're twenty eight
you take a chance to gain your throne

Take a chance on faith
I was just a lonely boy

forgive me father I sinned
forgive me father I will know
I will know
I will know

Walls

Don't you think it's time
That we both settle down
In a quiet little town
Beside the sea

The sky seems to be falling
And this road we keep on walking
We'll find a way to shelter from the rain

But You and I don't know
This road and where it goes
And honesty seems to go along way
So let me know you're safe
And we'll reach for a better place
And in my heart we will always stay

But it's a little late for promises
And time seems to be robbing us
of a life I know that we should have lived
when the world runs out of answers
I'll climb this Rocky ladder
and reach over this wall that's in the way

Don't you think it's time
that we both settle down
in a quiet little town and ride the train
It's been Cloudy in the morning
 And this road we keep on walking
We'll find a way to shelter from the rain

But You and I Both don't know
This road and where it goes
Or how much sunlight is left today
So let me know you're safe
And will reach for a better place
In my heart we will always stay

But It's a little late for promises
And time seems to be robbing us
Of a life I know that we should have lived
 When the world runs out of answers
and whatever fate will hand us

I will reach over this wall it's in the way

Don't you think this time
that we both settle down
in a quiet little town beside the sea

Eternity:

Water falls upon my face
As rain clouds shed a tear
All I have is who you are
Are all I hope there's you are near

I wait here a setting sun
For you to see me so
A penny for your thoughts
for a southern breeze to blow

And time is an Eternity
It was painted on the walls
Near city streets and payment tiles
Were the summer meets the fall
And for it is and we must trust
Another night to bide

Our dreams of truth a rising moon
Forever is a long long time

And words of wise
They tell the tale
That never seems to call
For we once were the destitute
And fate will write the law
We wonder the Pacific sky
As the Sun light turns it's back

As a cold dark nights will hide the moon
As the trees will turn to black

And time is an eternity
It was painted on the streets
Near city walls and payment tiles
To turn the grey complete

And for it is and we must trust
Another year to bide
Our dreams of truth
A rising moon
Forever is a long long time
Forever never dies
Forever I shall wait
An Eternity of moon and stars

forever I shall wait

Forever is a broken mile
Forever is eternal fate
A Destiny of moons and stars
Forever I shall wait

And time is an eternity
It was painted on the walls
Near city streets and payment Tiles
Where the sun light meets the fall

And for it is and we must trust
Another year to bid
Our dreams of truth a rising moon.
Forever is a long long time
Forever is a long-lived time
Forever is the question why

Forever You:

For you are my truth
My heart forever you
Daylight in my eyes
A sunset painted sky

Valleys, distant Hills
Follow nights of still
Coloured sands of time
I paint you in my mind

I need you now again
A compass to the sea
Eternal shores, open doors like a feather to the breeze
Stay with me once more, forever I adore
Your smile, your grace, your eyes
For you I'd wait the tides

My heart falls upon the waves
My heart must guide the end of the days

For I wait to see you through my mind
Will travel through time
My heart crossed the sea and the sands
Through hills and distant lands
Forever more unlocks the door to grace your hand in mine

For you are my truth
My heart forever you
The nights will surely bide
My moon will move the tide

The clock upon our wall
Eternal evermore
Sheets of times in lace
Eternal forever grace

With you
Forever you
Forever You

Waters and Waves. PI

You won't find me out in the big city
There's allot of shame
It's allot of pitty
You'll find me out in small town near the water and waves
Some people tell me I've been wasting my life
You gotta have some kids
you gotta get a wife
But it takes a while out here near the waters and waves

And life's a funny thing
You meet strangers down the road
Everywhere you go
And they all got a lot of things to say
Out here near the water is in waves

The sun beats down on my burnt back
I wish the road would cut me some slack
There's not allot going on down here near the waters and waves

And out here its gets pretty lonely
And I miss my baby back home in the big city
you gotta find some things to do from day to day

But as long as I got my guitar in my hand
And as long as I got the earth in the land
As long as the got the beaches to see the sand and the waters in waves

I'll sit here and sing my song
For how long I don't know for how long
But you know it'll be doing
I'll be seeing the sand the earth and the waves

Waters and Waves: PII

I spent the days of my youth trying to cope
With a whisky in hand and a fire to stoke
I feel the midday sun burning on my back again

I spend my nights on the road trying to shield
The cold dark clouds, fall in the field
That hide the moonlight I search for everyday

I travelled the road switching gears
The road less Travelled from years and years
And if I find another way I'll tell you everyday

And days of old will forever be
A certain clue, a destiny
A place in time that we will always stay

So wait for me, wait for us
Hold on to a place that we can trust
Where the wind is calm out here near the water and waves

Near the waters and waves
Near the waters and waves

Train wreck:

I'm packing in
I'm sipping blood
I'll take this fire out to the flood

I'm a rolling dice
my bones are aching
The storm is here no prisoners taken

Fire and Flames
You join the cult
Enjoy the pain like a lightning bolt

No end in sight
Have no fear
The spiders bite so hold my beer

I'm at Deadset Train wreck
Straight through the fire off the eastern coast off the eastern coast
I'm at Deadset Train wreck
Straight through the fire off the western coast off the western coast

I'm packing in
I'm sitting blood
I'll take this fire out to the flood

I'm a rolling dice
I'm flipping cards
I'm shaking whisky in the bar

There ain't no shame
If you join a mistaken
Guilty game of the Cult of Satan

I'm at Deadset Train wreck
Straight through the fire off the eastern coast off the eastern coast
I'm at Deadset Train wreck
Straight through the fire off the western coast off the western coast

I'm at Deadset Train wreck
Straight through the fire off the eastern coast off the eastern coast
I'm at Deadset Train wreck
Straight through the fire off the western coast off the western coast

Tides of San Diego:
I left my heart in San Diego
Packed my bags and hit the road
To a small old town by the mountains
With my heart to bear and load

She whispers me from San Diego
Golden hair and eyes of blue
From time to time I would set her free
Down by the caribou

I think about her all the time near the tide the San Diego
That's where my heart resides
I think about her every night near the tide the San Diego
I think about her as the years and waves roll by

I left my heart in San Diego
Pack my bags and filled the tank
to a small old town by the mountains
to share a beer with hank

I wandered round from year-to-year
Wasting light and talking cheap
Until the flood gates shut sometimes
And I never seemed to earn my keep

I think about her all the time near the tide the San Diego
That's where my heart resides
I think about her every night near the tide the San Diego
I think about her as the years and waves roll by

I Play Every Song For You:

I play every song for you
Baby it's you and me
And if they don't like it
It's time to set them free

Sometimes life's full of heartache
Sometimes we just survive
With you baby most of the time it's good to be alive

And I damn well won't back down

There's always another song
There's always another chance
And if you don't mind babe
I'd like your hand to dance

We tiptoe on the clouds
Sometimes just fall back down
But don't you worry about a thing
Because I play every song for you

There's always another chance
There's always another song
And sometimes I just don't know why people don't get along
It's getting kind of loud
And rowdy in the crowd
With my flag to bear
My cross to wear
My father would be proud

And I damn well won't back down

There's always another song
There's always another chance
And if you don't mind babe
I'd like your hand to dance

We tiptoe on the clouds
Sometimes just fall back down
But don't you worry about a thing
Because I play every song for you

Out here in the cold
I wanna stay with you 'till we're grey and old

There's always another song
There's always another chance
And if you don't mind babe
I'd like your hand to dance

We tiptoe on the clouds
Sometimes just fall back down
But don't you worry about a thing
Because I play every song for you

Huckleberry Finn (Letters to Heaven)

Hi Dad it's me
I'm sure you're quite aware
It's been a long old year
I know you're somewhere out there

I kind of made a mess of things
I'm not sure who to blame
But life is getting short
And I'm going quiet insane

Forgive me Dad I think of you every single day
Next time I know I'm doing wrong
I know who to blame

Forgive me Dad I think of you every single year
Next time I know I'm doing wrong
I'll walk right through the fear

My daughters far away
I'm going straight through hell
The one that thought that I had
Is empty by the shelf

I kind of think some pity
Will give me courage to myself
But life is getting long
A mental messing hell

So if I make it through this week
I'll be one of myself
I fear the anger my bones, my skin
My father's messing hands

And I don't know where the truth will messing lie
When I get my faith ill make it right

In another life
I will make it on my own
But when you're twenty eight
you take a chance to gain your throne

Take a chance on faith
I was just a lonely boy

forgive me father I sinned
forgive me father I will know
I will know
I will know

Credits:
Luke John Ingram
Samantha Rhiannon
Luke Owen's Country Mile
John Rhiannon
C: 2021